OCT 2 4 2003

 **W9-CTB-446**

21ST CENTURY DEBATES

WATER SUPPLY

OUR IMPACT ON THE PLANET

ROB BOWDEN

RAINTREE
STECK-VAUGHN
RSVP PUBLISHERS

A Harcourt Company

Austin   New York
www.raintreesteckvaughn.com

21st Century Debates Series

Genetics • Surveillance • Internet • Media • Artificial Intelligence • Climate Change • Energy • Rainforests • Waste, Recycling and Reuse • Endangered Species • Air Pollution • An Overcrowded World? • Food Supply • World Health • Third World Debt • Drugs • Terrorism • Transport

Library of Congress Cataloging-in-Publication Data is available upon request.

ISBN 0-7398-5506-9

Printed in Hong Kong. Bound in the United States.

1 2 3 4 5 6 7 8 9 0 LB 07 06 05 04 03 02

Picture acknowledgments: Associated Press 48 (Jassim Mohammed); Rob Bowden 17; James Davis Travel Photography (James Davis Worldwide) 8, 11, 57; Ecoscene 5 (Anthony Cooper), 18 (Christina Osborne), 32 (Nick Hawkes), 38 (David McHugh), 40 (Angela Hampton), 43 (Chinch Gryniewicz); Eye Ubiquitous 4 (NASA), 12 (Steve Brock), 47 (Julia Waterlow), 54 (Vidal); HWPL 7 and 16 (Jimmy Holmes), 13, 25, 49, cover foreground (Bennett Dean), cover background (Paul Thompson); Panos Pictures 14 (Giacomo Pirozzi), 44 (Trygve Bolstad); Edward Parker 22, 41; Popperfoto 27, 28 (R. Ezer), 31 (Gregg Newton), 34 (Rafiqur Rahman), 36 (Sukree Sukplang), 51 (George Mulala), 52 (Enamul Huq), 55 (Shawn Baldwin), 58 (Savita Kirloskar), 59 (Kevin Lamarque); Still Pictures 19, 24 and 42 (Mark Edwards), 20 (Shehzad Noorani), 30 (Ray Pfortner), 35 (M. & C. Denis-Huot), 45 (Bittu Sahgal), 56 (Gil Moti); Topham 23 (Carl J. Single); *Tuscaloosa News* 10 (Joe Oliveira); Zul Chapel Studios 39 (John Heinrich).

Cover: foreground picture shows two girls fetching water from a pipe in Xinjiang, China; background picture shows a hotel swimming pool in Montreal, Canada.

CONTENTS

A THIRSTY WORLD

A Blue Planet

"We drink it, we generate electricity with it, we soak our crops with it. And we're stretching our supplies to breaking point. Will we have enough clean water to satisfy all the world's needs?"

Peter Gleick, director, Pacific Institute for Studies in Development, Environment, and Security

FACT

If spread evenly over the entire planet, water would cover it to a depth of 1.5 miles (2.5 km).

If you could see Earth from space, you might be tempted to rename our planet "Water" because it is certainly very blue. In fact, water makes up almost 71 percent of Earth's surface, so all of the world's land area could fit into the Pacific Ocean, with 10 percent to spare! In addition to covering a vast area, water also covers the planet to an incredible depth. The Pacific Ocean, for example, has an average depth of 2.6 miles (4.2 km), while the Atlantic and Indian Oceans average around 2.3 miles (3.7 km). So why, with so much water around, do experts talk of water supplies running short? And why are they worried about having enough to meet everyone's needs in the future?

Water clearly dominates Earth, as viewed from space.

The Wrong Type of Water

The problem is that we require freshwater for most of our needs (drinking, agriculture, industry, etc.), but 97.5 percent of the water on Earth is salt water. Furthermore, less than 0.6 percent of Earth's freshwater (or 0.01 percent of all water) is actually available for human use. With an ever-expanding human population, the freshwater available per person is gradually declining. In 1900, for example, the global average stood at around 1,060,000 cubic feet per person, but by the year 2000 this had fallen to around 230,000 cubic feet. And if population growth continues as expected, then the global availability of freshwater could fall as low as 170,000 cubic feet per person by 2025.

Sprinklers water grass dividers in Palm Desert, California, suggesting that water is plentiful.

Despite this decline, it has been estimated that—if evenly distributed and used in a sustainable manner—available freshwater supplies could support a population up to three times larger than at present. So why, in the early 21st century, does one-sixth of the world's population (around 1 billion people) lack safe water?

Water Distribution

Water shortages often occur because of the way water is distributed. At a global level, Asia has the greatest annual availability of freshwater, while Australia and Oceania have the least. However, to fully understand the problems, it is necessary to consider the water available for each member of the population (per capita) within an area. From this point of view, Asia actually has the lowest availability of freshwater because of its enormous population. Australia and Oceania, by contrast, have the highest per capita supplies of freshwater because of their low populations.

Water supplies also vary at the regional and local levels. For instance, in some parts of the world even a single village can have very different levels of water availability from one end of its main street to the other. These differences in distribution are considered in greater detail in the next chapter.

Not Just Quantity

The water supply debate is not just about the quantity of water available. The quality of water also matters a great deal, as it has a direct impact on human health. In fact, illnesses related to unclean water and poor sanitation (lack of water for washing and toilets) cause the deaths of over 9,000 children every day—the biggest cause of death in the world. Almost all these deaths occur in developing countries, and they are nearly all preventable.

The most common cause of contaminated water is inadequate sanitation systems to dispose of waste water. Of particular concern is waste water that contains human waste, more commonly known as sewage. In 2000, the United Nations (UN) estimated that nearly 2.5 billion people lacked adequate sanitation, most of them living in rural areas in developing regions such as sub-Saharan Africa and South Asia.

Tubewells or boreholes, such as this one in Tamil Nadu, India, access groundwater. They can greatly improve the quality of local water supplies.

Water Use

Even where the quantity and quality of water are sufficient, water supply is a vitally important issue. Vast quantities of water are wasted in daily activities, and in some parts of the world supplies are getting dangerously low. In extreme cases, concern about water supplies even threatens to turn into conflict, as nations and different users compete for their share.

DEBATE

Before you read on, think about the different ways you use water in your own daily life. Then see how many of them come up in the rest of the book.

WATER AS A RESOURCE

A Drop in the Bucket

Much of Earth's freshwater is stored in glaciers, like this one in Everest National Park, Nepal.

As we have already seen, only 2.5 percent of Earth's water consists of freshwater. The bulk of this freshwater is locked up in ancient stores such as glaciers and snowfields or as groundwater in aquifers. Some of the water contained in these stores may be hundreds of thousands, even millions of years old, but only a small proportion of it is available for human use.

Our main sources of water are lakes, rivers, shallow aquifers, and water contained as moisture in soils, but not all the water held in these sources is usable. In reality, the amount used by humans is barely a "drop in the bucket." But for us, it is a very significant "drop."

A Renewable Resource?

In one sense, water can be seen as a renewable resource because it is constantly replenished as part of the global water cycle (see diagram). However, the reality is a little more complex, because not all water used by humans is instantly replaced. This is especially true of groundwater reserves, or aquifers. These can take thousands of years to replenish, since the water first has to penetrate (pass through) layers of soil and rock to reach the aquifer. Much of the world's freshwater is, in fact, stored in the ground below a level known as the water table. As rainfall seeps into the ground, it adds to this. In a period of prolonged rainfall, the water table can rise to the surface, causing flooding. However, the water table can also fall—during a dry period or if groundwater is removed.

FACT

Human diversion of freshwater using reservoirs and dams has caused a small but measurable change in the wobble of Earth as it spins.

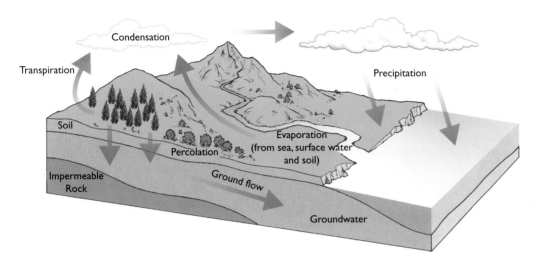

In parts of China, India, and the United States, groundwater is being pumped out faster than it is renewed, making it a nonrenewable resource in these places. Human actions, especially since the 1950s, have also altered the natural water cycle—often in dramatic ways. In the U.S., for example, half the annual river flow can be captured and stored in a network of over 70,000 dams. In deciding how renewable water is as a resource, it is therefore important to consider how long it takes for the water to be naturally replenished and the effects of any human interference on the water cycle.

Water is continually renewed through the water cycle.

All water on Earth	percent
Oceans	97.5
Freshwater	2.5
Freshwater resources on Earth:	
Glaciers, permanent snowcover	68.7
Fresh groundwater	30.054
Ground ice, permafrost	0.86
Freshwater lakes	0.26
Soil moisture	0.05
Atmospheric water vapor	0.04
Marshes, wetlands	0.03
Rivers	0.006

Source: The World's Water 2000–2001

VIEWPOINTS

"When humans use water at rates that exceed natural renewal rates, that is unsustainable."

Peter Gleick, The World's Water 2000–2001

"Although water is a renewable resource, the quantity of natural water on Earth is also limited and highly vulnerable to the effects of human action."

The World Guide 1999–2000, Instituto Del Tercer Mundo, Uruguay

VIEWPOINT

"Water supplies are distributed unevenly around the globe, with some areas containing abundant water and others a much more limited supply."
World Resources Institute. Pilot Analysis of Global Ecosystems: Freshwater Systems. 2000

Water Shortages

Seasonal shortages of water can occur almost anywhere in the world, affecting even well-watered nations such as the U.S., which often imposes water-use restrictions in times of drought. However, some countries suffer more permanent water shortages, particularly where the climate is naturally very dry, as in the Middle East and parts of Africa. These countries are said to suffer "water stress," a term used to describe a relative shortage of freshwater. Water stress measures the amount of water used (withdrawn) by a country, compared to the renewable freshwater available, using the following scale:

- **Low water stress**
  Less than 10 percent of total water available is used
- **Moderate water stress**
  10–20 percent of total water available is used
- **Medium to high water stress**
  20–40 percent of total water available is used
- **High water stress**
  More than 40 percent of total water available is used

Around a third of the world's population already lives in countries with moderate to high water stress (where 10–40+ percent of available water is used). If current trends in population growth and water use continue, this will increase to two-thirds of the world's population by 2025. The worst-affected areas are Africa and the Middle East, where some people barely have enough water for the basic requirements of drinking, cooking, and washing. In other countries, such as China, India, and Indonesia, water shortages are rapidly becoming a barrier to economic development.

A farmer fetches water for his horses during a very severe drought.

Water was used as a form of power in early economies. These Roman water wheels in Syria would have raised water from the river into the aqueducts behind them.

Water and the Economy

Water is needed for virtually everything we produce, use, or consume. Since its early use in the development of the steam engine (which powered the Industrial Revolution in 19th-century Europe and North America), water has played a central role in the world economy. Large industries, such as steel, paper, and textiles, are particularly dependent on having access to large quantities of water for their production processes. This is why they are often located close to rivers or other water sources.

Humans use water mainly for agriculture, particularly for the irrigation of crops.

The world's industries account for 22 percent of global freshwater use, but this is expected to double by 2025. In rapidly industrializing nations, such as China, it could increase by up to five times.

By far the biggest user of water, however, is agriculture. Farming accounts for 70 percent of global use, and around 90 percent of use in the mainly rural economies of Africa and southern Asia. Most of this water is used to irrigate cropland that provides roughly 40 percent of the world's food. In fact, it is irrigation that has helped us avoid the food shortages predicted in the 1950s and 1960s. However, as population continues to grow, and industry demands a greater share of water resources, some experts are concerned that there may not be sufficient water for agriculture in the future.

Domestic use (in the home) consumes the least water globally, at just 8 percent on average. But in more developed countries, the percentage is generally much higher. In Denmark, Sweden, and New Zealand, for example, domestic water use accounts for over 30 percent of consumption.

Valuing Water

Despite its importance, water is often undervalued as a resource. You rarely hear news reports about the price of water, yet a change in gasoline prices always makes the headlines. The problem is that many people take water for granted; they see it fall as rain, fill their rivers, and flow from their sinks on demand. The situation is very different for millions living in developing regions. There, many people (especially women and children) may walk several miles just to get enough to drink each day. Such people could teach those who take it for granted some important lessons in appreciating water as the precious resource—the so-called "blue gold"—that it is.

VIEWPOINTS

"Today we continue to ignore the vital importance of water, while consuming more and more."
Julie Stauffer, The Water Crisis

"In this new century, water, its sanitation, and its equitable distribution pose great social challenges for our world. We need to safeguard the global supply of healthy water and to ensure that everyone has access to it."
Kofi Annan, secretary-general, United Nations

At the same time, however, those with minimal water should be provided with more plentiful supplies, closer to their homes, in order to improve their standard of living. This presents a difficult challenge for governments and communities, but learning to value water more highly than it is at present would be a positive first step.

FACT

It has been reported that wells drilled around Beijing, China, now have to reach 3,300 feet (1,000 meters) deep to tap freshwater, adding dramatically to the cost of supply.

Percentage water use by type, 2000

Country	Agriculture	Industry	Domestic
Australia	75%	10%	15%
Brazil	40%	17%	43%
China	77%	18%	5%
Denmark	43%	27%	30%
India	92%	3%	5%
Japan	64%	17%	19%
Kenya	76%	4%	20%
South Africa	72%	11%	17%
United Kingdom	3%	77%	20%
United States	42%	46%	12%

Key ☐ Agriculture ☐ Industry ■ Domestic

Source: The World's Water 2000-2001

Water, the so-called "blue gold," tumbles over Seven Stream Falls, Agbokim, Nigeria.

DEBATE

Why is water such an important resource and how can we appreciate it more in the future? What information do you think you should be given about your own domestic water supplies and how would it be useful?

WATER IS LIFE

A Basic Human Right

Oral rehydration salts are given to treat diarrhea, usually caused by drinking contaminated water.

Water is essential for sustaining life, not just for humans, but for all living things. While some plants and animals are able to survive for long periods without water, the average human would live just three days, and in some hotter climates maybe only a matter of hours.

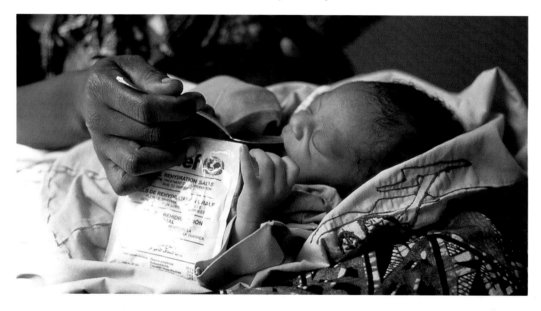

Water is also considered a basic human right, essential for our health and development. However, the many international agreements covering human rights since 1948 have largely ignored the right to water, perhaps because it seems so obvious—a bit like our right to air. The problem is that not everyone has access to water. For millions of others, the quantity and quality of water available is insufficient to meet their needs. For this reason, some experts believe that water should be recognized as a basic human right—in the same way as food, shelter, and protection. But it is impossible to give people the right to unlimited amounts of water, especially in those countries or regions that suffer natural shortages. So how much water is necessary to meet basic human needs?

How Much Is Enough?

As an absolute minimum, humans require .8–1.3 gallons (3–5 litres) of clean water per day in order to survive. However, studies have shown that overall human health is improved if this is increased to around 5.25 gallons (20 l) per person (capita) per day (gpcd). This amount allows enough for basic sanitation and hygiene, in addition to drinking water. But water is also used for bathing and for preparing and cooking food. If these are included, then a figure of 13 gpcd (50 lpcd) has been recommended as a more realistic minimum to meet basic needs.

Sixty-two countries, including Kenya, India, Jamaica, and Albania, with a total population of some 2.2 billion people, reported having less than 13 gpcd (50 lpcd) available in the year 2000. Another 39 countries reported having less than half the recommended minimum, while the lowest, Gambia and Haiti, reported just .8 gpcd (3 lpcd)—barely enough water to survive.

Recommended basic water requirement for human domestic needs

Purpose	Gallons per capita per day (lpcd)
Drinking water	1.3
Sanitation	5.25
Bathing	4
Food preparation/cooking	2.6
Total	13.15

Source: The World's Water 2000–2001

VIEWPOINTS

"Access to safe water is a fundamental human need and, therefore, a basic human right."
Kofi Annan, secretary-general, United Nations

"While access to clean water and sanitation, as one of the most basic human needs, is today considered part of people's human rights, it has yet to be incorporated into the Universal Declaration of Human Rights."
WaterAid, Great Britain

FACT

The average U.S. citizen uses 130 gallons (500 l) of water per day. In Great Britain, the daily average is about 53 gallons (200 l) per person.

Open sewers, shown here in Kuala Lumpur, Malaysia, are a breeding ground for water-related diseases.

However, national water shortage figures can be misleading. They do not show the variations in water availability within a country or even in a single town or city. For example, those living in urban areas are likely to have much more than 13 gpcd (50 lpcd) of water available, while some rural populations may have considerably less. In rural areas, moreover, people often meet their domestic water needs from wells, boreholes, and rivers, and this type of supply may be ignored in reported figures. Most importantly, water supply figures do not always include information about water quality.

This means that some countries may appear to have sufficient water to meet their basic requirements but the water may not be of good-enough quality to be usable.

Water and Health

Clean water is vital to our health, and many of the world's greatest health problems are caused by a lack of clean water. Diarrhea is by far the most serious threat to human health and accounted for over 2.2 million deaths in 1998, most of which would have been avoided if clean water and safe sanitation facilities had been available.

Diarrheal diseases are spread when water becomes contaminated with bacteria and parasites from human waste, which are then transmitted to the people using that water. This is a serious problem in many rural areas that lack proper disposal methods for human waste and in fast-growing cities (mainly in developing countries) where sewage systems cannot cope with the sheer volume of human waste generated. Poor personal hygiene, when people fail to wash their hands after going to the toilet and then prepare or consume food, also spreads these diseases. Simply washing your hands with soap and water has been proven to reduce incidence of diarrhea by 35 percent.

Cholera and typhoid are also spread by contaminated water. Cholera has been a particular problem following natural disasters such as floods or earthquakes, when water supplies can easily become contaminated as sewage systems overflow or are damaged. In Madagascar, over 700 people were killed and 10,000 infected by an outbreak of cholera after extreme flooding there in March 2000.

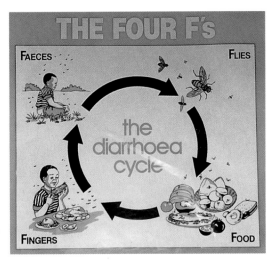

A Kenyan health poster shows patients how diarrhea is transmitted.

VIEWPOINT

"Water resource programs for power generation and irrigation have resulted in ...outbreaks of schistosomiasis in several African countries."
World Health Organization

Water-Related Diseases

Not all water-related diseases are caused by drinking contaminated water or poor hygiene. Others, such as malaria and schistosomiasis (or bilharzia), are caused by organisms that rely on water for their survival. Malaria is a parasite carried by mosquitoes that depend on water to breed and lay their eggs. This makes those living close to water in malarial countries (mainly in the tropics) extremely vulnerable. Malaria kills over one million people each year and causes suffering for millions more.

Bilharzia is another water-based parasite, carried by a small snail that lives in slow-moving or still water in tropical countries. The parasite passes through human skin when people enter contaminated water and lays thousands of eggs, which then spread into the intestines and bladder. Bilharzia causes anemia, internal scarring, liver damage, and diarrhea, and also leads to a loss of energy and extreme tiredness.

Some 200 million people are affected by bilharzia, and it is thought to kill around 200,000 each year. Drugs can provide a cure but many people become re-infected soon afterward. A more effective (but also expensive) control is to kill the snails carrying bilharzia, using pesticides. Bilharzia is especially associated with irrigation ditches that provide an ideal breeding ground for snails carrying the parasite.

Irrigation ditches often increase water-related diseases. This project is in Sudan.

Countries like Egypt, Sudan, Tanzania, and Ghana have experienced dramatic increases in those infected with bilharzia from between 0–10 percent, before irrigation was introduced, to around 40 percent (and as high as 75–90 percent) afterward. The problem is that irrigation ditches are vital to provide food and crops and cannot simply be abandoned. One solution, many experts agree, is to educate people better about water-related diseases and how to avoid them.

In developing countries, up to 90 percent of sewage is untreated. This sewage outlet is in Mexico City.

Deaths from water-related diseases in 1998

Disease	Deaths
Diarrheal diseases	2,219,000
Malaria	1,110,000
Intestinal worm infections	17,000

Source: WHO 1999 World Health Report

The Importance of Education

Many of the countries that suffer most from water-related diseases are also among the poorest and least-educated nations of the world. In such countries, education is widely considered the most important tool in the fight to reduce and eventually eliminate many water-related diseases.

These Bangladeshi women are learning about safe water supply.

Even in areas where water supply and sanitation are still lacking, teaching people about ways of reducing the risk of infection has proved to be very effective. For example, incidences of infection with the Guinea worm parasite, which affects India and Central and West Africa, fell by over 97 percent (from 3.5 million to 150,000 cases) during the 1990s. This was despite relatively little improvement in water supplies and sanitation. The reduction was mainly due to people being taught about the disease and being shown how to use cloth filters to stop the Guinea worm from getting into their drinking water.

Teaching people about the importance of washing their hands after using the toilet, and before eating or preparing food or collecting water, has also led to dramatic reductions in diarrhea throughout the world. This shows that educating people to change their behavior is just as important as technology is in solving water-related health problems.

Providing Water for All?

In developed countries, water is normally carried into homes and businesses through a network of pipes. It is then carried away again, as sewage, for treatment and eventual disposal. However, such systems are expensive to operate. In many developing countries, governments find the costs virtually impossible to meet, especially as their populations tend to grow very rapidly, putting even more pressure on their public water systems.

The resulting shortfall in supply is increasingly being made up by private companies who charge homeowners for clean water and sanitation services. In Lima, Peru, the majority of households rely on private suppliers, and in some West African cities such services are used by up to 85 percent of the population.

As private suppliers are normally more expensive than state systems, critics are concerned that water —the most basic human requirement—could be too expensive for some if it becomes privatized. Others believe that private operators charge a more realistic price for water and sanitation, and are better able to meet local needs and the target of providing water for all. Sewage treatment systems are especially costly. A cheaper alternative, used in much of the developing world, is on-site pit latrines.

VIEWPOINTS

"...in many urban areas poor people are forced to pay exorbitant prices for low-quality dirty water from small-scale private vendors."
Tearfund/WaterAid "Water Matters" campaign

"Although local suppliers can be more expensive than public providers, households would be worse off without them ... In many countries small informal water vendors and sanitation providers reach poor urban areas unserved by government utilities."
World Bank. World Development Report 2000-2001

DEBATE

Think about your own consumption of water. If you were limited to less than 5.25 gallons (20 l), or one large bucket, per day (as many people in the world are), how would it affect your daily life?

THE WELL RUNS DRY

Under Pressure

During the last century, population increased by around 365 percent, reaching a total of just over 6 billion by 2000. In that same time, however, the amount of water withdrawn from rivers, aquifers, and other water sources increased by over 900 percent, placing water resources under extreme pressure. Now politicians and planners everywhere are starting to take water-supply problems seriously. And their concern is justified because there are clear warning signs that, for many, the well is already running dry.

Aquifer Depletion

One of the greatest signs of declining water availability is aquifer depletion—the unsustainable use of groundwater reserves. Globally, up to 2 billion people depend on groundwater for their primary source of drinking water and many more depend indirectly on groundwater that is extracted to support agriculture or industry. In the United States, for example, 43 percent of irrigated farmland relies on water pumped from aquifers. Meanwhile in India, the number of tubewells used to extract groundwater for irrigation grew from 3,000 in 1960 to 6 million by 1990, increasing the area irrigated by 113 times!

The Basilica de Guadalupe, Mexico City, is slowly sinking due to groundwater overextraction.

Such enormous increases in groundwater extraction have had a major impact on aquifers, because in many cases the rate of withdrawal has been higher than their natural replenishment. The problem is particularly severe because the average time it takes groundwater to be recycled is 1,400 years (as opposed to just 20 days for river water). Mexico City, the capital of Mexico and one of the biggest cities in the world, has seen water levels in its aquifer fall by over 32 feet (10 m). As a result, parts of Mexico City have suffered land sinking of up to 30 feet (9 m) as the land sinks into the gap left by the extracted water. Similar problems are found in Bangkok, Thailand, Venice, Italy, and many other cities. One problem is that, as the land sinks, it compacts the ground, meaning that the aquifer may never be restored even if water extraction has stopped.

FACT

More than 95 percent of the rural population in the United States depends on groundwater for drinking.

Drilling is needed to reach falling water tables in the town of Otisco, New York.

Groundwater used as drinking water, by region, late 1990s

Region	Percentage of drinking water from groundwater	Population dependent on groundwater (millions)
Asia-Pacific	32	1,000–1,200
Europe	75	200–500
Latin America	29	150
United States	51	135
Australia	15	3
Africa	no data	no data

Source: State of the World 2001

Saltwater Intrusion

Another result of overextraction from aquifers, especially near coastal areas, is saltwater intrusion from the sea into groundwater supplies. Where groundwater is extracted too rapidly, the natural flow of water from land to sea can be reversed, leading to saltwater draining into the depleted aquifers. In the Mediterranean region of Europe, for example, 53 out of 126 aquifers were suffering from saltwater intrusion in 1999, with Spain, Italy, and Turkey experiencing the most cases. Florida, Israel, and the state of Gujarat in India are among other regions battling with the problems of drinking water contaminated by saltwater.

As little as 2 percent of saltwater in a freshwater aquifer can make it unsuitable for human use. And even inland areas can suffer when saltwater held in deep aquifers rises to replace that being extracted from the shallower groundwater supplies. This has occurred in parts of Eastern Europe, including Latvia, Poland, and Moldova. Saltwater intrusion is especially troubling because the problems it causes cannot be quickly resolved, if at all.

Drilling for groundwater in Jordan. Groundwater extraction can lead to saltwater intrusion if the groundwater is removed too rapidly.

This desert region of Saudi Arabia is typical of much of the Middle East region. In such dry places, groundwater can be the only hope of finding freshwater supplies.

It seriously disrupts local water supplies, not only affecting drinking water but also the irrigation systems needed to grow crops, at a time when water for agriculture is already under great threat.

Water for Agriculture

Agriculture accounts for about 70 percent of global water use at present, and its use in irrigation has been a vital factor in meeting the increased global demand for food over the last 50 years. However, as food supplies become a major focus of attention, there are grave concerns about whether there is enough water to produce sufficient food to feed the world's growing population. Experts estimate that, in order to meet the food needs of a predicted 8 billion people in 2025, water supplies need to increase by the equivalent of 10 Niles—the world's longest river—per year! This seems an almost impossible target, given that almost a tenth of current food is produced on farms that are using groundwater unsustainably. Furthermore, many rivers already have so much water diverted for irrigation that they no longer reach the sea for part of the year. These include the Colorado river (which runs from Colorado to the Gulf of California), the Nile, and the Ganges.

VIEWPOINTS

"Severe water scarcity presents the single biggest threat to future food production. Even now, many freshwater sources—underground aquifers and rivers—are stressed beyond their limits."
Sandra Postel, director, Global Water Policy Project, Massachusetts

"Without...irrigation water, the food produced by natural precipitation would be insufficient to feed the world's current population."
Peter Gleick, director, Pacific Institute for Studies in Development, Environment, and Security

There is also the added pressure of greater competition for water to meet growing domestic and industrial demands. Water used for industry is up to 70 times more economically productive than water used for agriculture, and it creates more jobs. In California, for example, the same amount of water needed to support 100,000 high-tech jobs would support fewer than ten jobs in agriculture.

Changes in people's diets are also having a dramatic impact on water availability. In North America, for instance, high-calorie diets including large quantities of meat require around 1,300 gallons (5,000 l) of water per person per day to produce. In South Asia and sub-Saharan Africa, by comparison, around 555 gallons (2,100 l) and 465 gallons (1,760 l) respectively are needed to produce the more vegetable- and grain-based diets of these regions. As diets in many parts of the world become similar to those of Americans, the impact on future water demands is considerable.

Growing More with Less

With declining supplies and increased competition for water, many experts believe that the only way agricultural production can increase is to improve irrigation efficiency. On many irrigated farms, less than half the water actually reaches the plants, the rest being lost in leakages, evaporation, or soaking up by surrounding soils. But if farmers use improved technology, such as low-energy sprinklers or drip irrigation, water losses can be reduced to less than 10 percent. Studies in India, Israel, Spain, and the United States also suggest that crop yields per acre (hectare) of land can increase by 20–90 percent when farmers switch from traditional flood irrigation (flooding water onto the fields) to drip systems.

Such technology is expensive, however, and requires computer-controlled systems to achieve maximum benefits. Many farmers, especially in developing countries, cannot afford such technology, and its use is often limited to producing high-quality export produce. In Kenya, for example, roses and other flowers are grown for export using computerized drip irrigation while people living within sight of the plantation struggle with water shortages and regularly depend on food relief.

VIEWPOINT

"We now eat more beef, pork, poultry, eggs, and dairy products, which in turn means a greater demand for grain to feed animals; more grain means more water is needed for irrigation."
TearfundWaterAid "Water Matters" campaign

The benefits of drip irrigation are explained by an Israeli scientist to agricultural experts from African countries, including Senegal and the Democratic Republic of the Congo. Israel is the world leader in this technology.

Average water requirements to produce 2.2 pounds (1kg) of different food

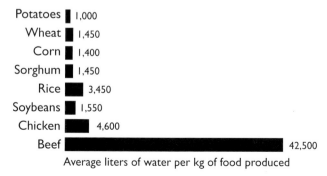

Food	Average liters of water per kg of food produced
Potatoes	1,000
Wheat	1,450
Corn	1,400
Sorghum	1,450
Rice	3,450
Soybeans	1,550
Chicken	4,600
Beef	42,500

Average liters of water per kg of food produced

Source: The World's Water 2000–2001

"If we could ever competitively, at a cheap rate, get freshwater from saltwater, that would be in the long-range interests of humanity [and] would dwarf any other scientific accomplishments."
John F. Kennedy, former U.S. president, 1961

"In the future, the water in your glass may have originated in the seas."
Diane Martindale, science writer

Increasing Water Supplies

Even if water-saving technologies were widely adopted in agriculture, many water-scarce countries would still have insufficient water to meet their needs. So instead, they are looking at ways of increasing their water supplies. Perhaps the most famous example is Libya's Great Manmade River, referred to by many as the eighth wonder of the world. It is the world's biggest water project and when complete (it started in 1984) will transfer water from the Kufra and Sareer aquifers 2,130 feet (650 m) under the Libyan desert to the main

A giant bag is lowered into the Mediterranean. It will be used to transport drinking water from Turkey to Cyprus.

population centers along Libya's coast via some 2,175 miles (3,500 km) of pipes. The water contained in the Kufra aquifer is said to be equivalent to 200 years' worth of the Nile river's flow and is intended to bring an agricultural revolution to Libya's people.

An alternative solution is desalination—obtaining freshwater from Earth's vast saltwater resources. In 2001, around 1 percent of global drinking water was supplied by 12,500 desalination plants, mainly in the Middle East, United States, Caribbean, and the Mediterranean areas. At present, Saudi Arabia, the U.S., the United Arab Emirates, and Kuwait account for 56 percent of global desalination capacity, but the technology is used by 120 countries in total and is expected to expand as freshwater gets scarcer and desalination technology becomes cheaper.

Desalination could be particularly beneficial to small islands with little natural freshwater. But another method (already used in some parts of the world) is to haul water in giant bags from places where it is more plentiful. This is how some Greek islands are supplied with water from mainland Greece during the peak tourist season and water has also been hauled from Turkey to Cyprus. The technology is still new and has suffered setbacks (such as bags ripping during their voyage), but the hope is that it might become another way to help countries—especially islands—overcome their water shortages.

Conserving Water

Unfortunately, existing methods of increasing water supplies are often expensive and may simply divert water from one place to another or offer short-term solutions. In the struggle to avoid the wells running dry, it is equally important that we make efforts to reduce human demand by conserving water. We will explore those issues shortly (see page 36).

FACT

In South Africa, 60 percent of water is used for irrigation by 600,000 white farmers, while 15 million black people lack direct access to water.

DEBATE

What are the main threats to the world's water supplies? What would you suggest planners should focus their attention on, to prevent the well from running dry?

POLLUTED WATER

Declining Water Quality

A long with growing water shortages, declining water quality is placing additional stress on the world's water supplies. In many parts of the world, drinking water already violates health guidelines set for various pollutants. And, because some pollutants take so long to enter the water cycle (especially groundwater), experts warn that the problem is likely to get worse even if action is taken immediately. Furthermore, humans continue creating and using more toxic and persistent chemicals. This means that, as fast as known pollutants are being treated (or, better yet, prevented from entering water supplies in the first place), new and more hazardous pollutants are emerging.

Domestic Pollutants

The most basic domestic pollutant is our own waste (sewage) which, as we have seen, can be a major source of disease if not properly disposed of. In the more developed nations, systems to treat and handle sewage have been in place for many years, and pollution and water-related disease has virtually disappeared. In developing countries, however, up to 90 percent of sewage may enter water systems without any treatment at all. This creates not only problems of pollution, but also conditions in which diseases can spread.

There was a dramatic example of this in Peru in 1991, when untreated sewage entered the sea, contaminating local seafood and leading to an outbreak of cholera. A total of 320,000 cases were

Leachate from a landfill in Washington. Leachate often contains toxic substances and it is a major water pollutant.

reported and almost 3,000 people died. The pollution also cost the economy an estimated $1 billion due to reduced tourism and canceled agricultural exports. This was more than three times what the government had spent on water and sanitation improvements in the previous ten years.

Developed nations are not completely immune from such problems, either. For example, in 1993, over 400,000 people in Milwaukee became infected with a parasite (*Cryptosporidium parvum*). The parasite had entered the city's water supplies when a water treatment plant failed to filter it out of the supply from Lake Michigan, the source of Milwaukee's water.

Besides human waste, domestic pollutants include the chemicals used in cleaning and personal hygiene products, with phosphates (chemical salts) from laundry soaps particularly causing serious problems.

VIEWPOINTS

"The declining state of freshwater resources may become the dominant issue for the 21st century's environment and development agenda."
Intermediate Technology Development Group

"The quality of surface waters in industrialized countries has generally been improving with respect to some pollutants over the last 20 years, but new chemicals are increasingly becoming a problem."
World Resources Institute. Pilot Analysis of Global Ecosystems: Freshwater Systems

Sewage released into the ocean threatens the health of surfers in Rio de Janeiro, Brazil.

The algae covering this drainage channel in Cambridgeshire, England, is probably caused by nitrate runoff from nearby farms.

If too many phosphates accumulate in lakes and rivers, they can cause a process called eutrophication, in which rapid plant and algae growth gradually robs the water of oxygen and blocks sunlight, causing aquatic life to die. The damage to aquatic ecosystems can eventually cause a decline in water quality, making it more expensive to treat. Many soap manufacturers have removed phosphates from their cleaning products in order to reduce this problem.

Agricultural Pollutants

Phosphates are also used as an agricultural fertilizer. But, with only 7–15 percent being absorbed by the plants, many phosphate fertilizers end up entering and polluting water systems. Nitrogen fertilizers are used even more widely and have caused water pollution incidents throughout the world.

FACT

Since the 1950s, the use of nitrogen fertilizers in agriculture has increased twentyfold.

In Denmark, which had one of the world's highest application rates of nitrogen fertilizers in 1990, levels of nitrate in groundwater supplies have tripled since the 1940s. Several other countries, including the U.S., Great Britain, China, and India, have also seen significant increases in nitrate pollution.

Besides eutrophication problems in lakes and rivers, high levels of nitrates can lead to a condition in humans called infant methemoglobinemia (or "blue baby syndrome") where the blood's ability to carry oxygen is limited. This is known to have killed some 3,000 babies, half of them in Hungary, since 1945. High nitrate levels have also been linked to higher chances of miscarriage among pregnant women.

Of greater concern perhaps are agricultural pesticides. These highly toxic substances have been used increasingly over recent decades. Some are still present in water samples taken today, despite being banned over thirty years ago. In sufficient quantities, pesticides have been linked to an increased risk of certain cancers and to genetic abnormalities in humans and animals.

In the past, natural processes in streams and brooks removed many agricultural pollutants before they reached main water sources. (Pollutants were dispersed into the soils or absorbed by aquatic plants such as reeds.) But nowadays, with the volume of pollutants growing and many streams being filled in, this natural control is no longer sufficient. The pollution problems could be eased by farmers reducing their use of agrochemicals and not planting crops close to waterways. However, under constant pressure to produce greater quantities of food, many farmers ignore such ideas. In most nations, agriculture therefore remains the biggest single source of water pollutants.

VIEWPOINTS

"If we restored and took care of all the small streams on the landscape, our water quality coming down rivers would be greatly improved."
Bruce Peterson. Marine Biological Laboratory. Woods Hole. Massachusetts

"Although a river can assimilate a certain amount of organic waste, it can't cope with huge volumes of sewage and it can't destroy every pathogen present in human waste."
Julie Stauffer. The Water Crisis

FACT

In the United States, farm animals produce 130 times more waste than humans.

VIEWPOINT

"We have reached the stage where the entire hydrosphere [all the world's surface and subsurface water], with the possible exception of the polar ice caps, is contaminated (at least to some extent) by our industrial pollutants."
Julie Stauffer, The Water Crisis

Industrial Pollutants

Although industrial pollutants may enter water supplies in lower quantities than agricultural and domestic pollutants, they are often more hazardous to both people and the environment. One of the problems with industrial pollutants is that we simply do not know enough about them. There are over 10 million synthetic chemicals in use today, with hundreds more being created every week. But we know nothing about the potential hazards of around 70 percent of them, and only around 2 percent have been fully tested.

Among the most serious industrial pollutants are heavy metals, such as cadmium, lead, and mercury, because they can interfere with human

reproduction and development. They also bioaccumulate as they pass through the food chain. This means that, by the time humans eat fish, for example, the doses of toxins can be very high. For instance, in Minamata, Japan, mercury dumped into the oceans by a local chemical factory bioaccumulated and led to people being poisoned when they ate local fish. Over 300 people died as a result of this incident, which alerted the world to the dangers of industrial water pollution.

Arsenic, which occurs naturally in Bangladesh's soils, has polluted local water supplies following the drilling of tubewells since the 1970s. Bangladesh's prime minister paints this tubewell red to warn that it is contaminated.

VIEWPOINT

"In many parts of the world, we are only just beginning to discover contamination caused by practices of 30 or 40 years ago."
Payal Sampat, WorldWatch Institute

Flamingos on Lake Nakuru, Kenya, are recovering as water pollution is reduced.

Pollutants and the Environment

Industrial pollutants are also extremely harmful to the environment, if they enter the water system. In Kenya's Lake Nakuru, for instance, thousands of flamingos have died as a result of water pollution from nearby battery and chemical factories. Thankfully, new water treatment systems are improving water quality and the flamingo population is now recovering.

Industrial accidents, such as oil spills, can cause some of the worst damage to aquatic environments. In January 2000, for example, cyanide used in a Romanian gold mine leaked into the Tisza River, killing nearly all the river's wildlife, which could take years to recover. Other pollutants become dissolved in rainwater and can therefore cause damage to environments hundreds of miles from their source. For instance, nitrogen and sulfur emitted from British industries and vehicles have caused widespread damage to lakes in Scandinavia, where it falls as acid rain and enters the water systems.

FACT

Cleaning up the 300,000–400,000 contaminated groundwater sites in the United States is expected to cost $1 trillion over a 30-year period.

DEBATE

What measures could you take as an individual to try to reduce water pollution in your own area?

WATER
CONSERVATION

A Double Challenge!

As we have seen, water resources are under increasing pressure from pollution as well as from rising demand. This means that we are faced with a double challenge:
- to conserve and protect aquatic environments from the effects of overconsumption and pollution
- to provide sufficient safe water to meet the needs of a growing human population

Thailand's worsening water shortages have caused some roads to crack, but villagers continue to extract water using mobile pumps.

It is not possible to separate the two issues—conservation and meeting growing demand—because they are interdependent. Where providing more water for human use has been the priority,

overextraction from aquifers has resulted in environmental decline and species loss. Ultimately, this could threaten future water supplies in many parts of the world.

In Spain's Upper Guadiana region, for example, the overextraction of groundwater has caused water levels to drop by 98–130 feet (30–40 m) and led to important wetland habitats drying out. And in Denmark, six important wetlands are threatened by groundwater overexploitation, a threat shared by 25 percent of Europe's major wetlands. Besides changing the natural water cycle, wetland damage can also harm the plants and wildlife that depend on them. In North America, for instance, 39 percent of plant species depend on wetlands, and they in turn support numerous birds and animals.

Reducing Consumption

The water supply debate often focuses on new ways of getting more water, but it is just as important, if not more so, to reduce demand for water in the first place. If existing supplies were used more efficiently, then more would be available for other uses and pressure on natural systems would be reduced. Reductions can be achieved by adopting new irrigation techniques in farming (as described on pages 26–27), but there is much that could be done in industry and around the home, too.

Some industries have already started making dramatic cuts in the water they consume. Before World War II, for example, a ton of steel required between 60 and 100 tons of water to produce, but today's technology has reduced water consumption to below 6 tons. Some car manufacturers have further reduced water consumption by making cars using aluminum instead of steel. Aluminum uses just 1.5 tons of water per ton.

FACT

It takes around 105,000 gallons (400,000 l) of water to make a single steel car.

VIEWPOINTS

"New technologies can help farmers around the world supply food for the growing population, while simultaneously protecting rivers, lakes, and aquifers."
Sandra Postel, director, Global Water Policy Project, Massachusetts

"Technology can help, but it cannot guarantee the right to water for the 1.4 billion people around the world who are today deprived of it."
Riccardo Petrella, The Water Manifesto, 2001

Conservation at Home

Globally, domestic water use currently accounts for much less than agriculture and industry, but proportionately its use is increasing due to population growth and the fact that more and more people are living in large towns and cities. This makes it all the more important to start using less water in our homes now.

Some relatively simple measures can make a significant difference without really affecting people's lifestyle. For example, flushing the toilet accounts for about 38 percent (more than a third) of the water used within the average home each day. This could be drastically reduced by using low-flow toilets that require up to 70 percent less water per flush. Since 1992, all new toilets in the United States have been designed as low-flow models and a similar law was passed in Great Britain in 1993. Some countries have taken more direct measures to force change. In Mexico City, for example, 350,000 old toilets were replaced with efficient new ones, and this saved enough water to supply an additional 250,000 residents.

This compost toilet uses no water at all. The waste is broken down into a natural rich compost. Some wood chippings or sawdust are added after each use to reduce smells. If well maintained, there is hardly any odor at all.

Washing vegetables under running water is very wasteful. Washing them in a bowl is less wasteful and the water can be re-used, to water a plant, for example.

Individual Action

We can all do a lot, as individuals, to conserve water. Washing machines, for instance, use a lot of water (up to 26 gallons (100 l) per load), so waiting until we have a full load means that water is used to its maximum efficiency. Modern washing machines reduce water use even further, so if your family buys a new one check to see how water-efficient it is. Many actions are even simpler, such as not flushing the toilet every time you use it, or turning off the faucet while you are brushing your teeth.

Hoses are particularly wasteful. If attached to a garden sprinkler, for example, they can use as much water in half an hour as an average family of four would in an entire day. A watering can or bucket uses much less water. If you must use a hose, then it's best to use it in the evening when the heat of the day has passed, to reduce water loss from evaporation. Many local water companies have further tips on water conservation, so contact them to find out more. Better still, think of your own ideas and tell others.

FACT

A shower uses about 60 percent less water than having a bath.

FACT

A faucet dripping once every second wastes about 1 gallon (4 l) of water per day.

Leaks in water systems waste valuable water, often after it has been treated.

Conservation Pays

Conservation not only saves water, but saves money. Less has to be spent on cleaning and treating water (normally to drinkable standards) that is then simply flushed down a toilet or used to water a lawn. This is important, because it means that governments and water companies have more money available to extend services or maintain existing networks at a higher standard. In many countries, over 30 percent of treated water is lost as a result of leaks in the water system. Even in wealthy countries such as the United States, which can afford to maintain their systems, it is common for about 10–20 percent of water to be lost in this way.

Consumers can also save money by using water more wisely. This is especially true if water is paid for by a meter, as it is in the United States. In Great Britain, farms and industries also pay for their water using meters, but many domestic homes pay a flat rate. The flat rate means that they can use as much water as they want and still pay the same amount. Such systems do not encourage water efficiency.

In Great Britain, all homes built since 1989 must have a water meter installed, and local water companies will install meters to older homes free of charge. Studies have shown that people then become less wasteful and can often save money compared with those paying a flat rate. There is some concern, however, that those who may need to use more water than most, such as the elderly or sick, could cut back on their use too much as a result of water meters. For most users, however, a meter has only positive effects, making them more aware of the water they use and encouraging water conservation.

Industries that improve water efficiency also benefit financially. In the United States, the electronics and pharmaceutical company 3M introduced a "pollution prevention pays" program in 1975. New manufacturing processes, many of which focused on reducing water use and pollution, succeeded in cutting waste water production by 1,412 million cubic feet or 1.4 billion cubic feet (40 million cubic meters) per year. In the first nine years, the company saved over $200 million, proving that water conservation really can pay.

VIEWPOINTS

"Why should communities raise all water to drinkable standards and then use that expensive resource for flushing toilets or watering lawns?"
Peter Gleick, director, Pacific Institute for Studies in Development, Environment, and Security

"When water is expensive, either in cash terms or in the time and energy needed to collect it, the poor often cut [reduce] total consumption."
World Bank, Water Sanitation and Poverty, 2001

Water meters are now a standard feature in many new houses. Regular readings encourage people to reduce their water consumption.

VIEWPOINT

"...the history of the collection of rainwater is as old as the history of mankind. The use of rainwater-collection systems is known to have existed 4,000 years ago."

Dr Adhityan Appan. president. International Catchment Systems Association

Water Harvesting

Another way of conserving water is to make better use of water that is naturally available. Such techniques are known as water harvesting and have been practiced for thousands of years in all parts of the world. One of the simplest methods is the use of small barriers made of stones or earth. These lines in fields (sometimes called bunds) trap rainwater behind them, forcing it to soak into the soil where it can then be used for farming. In Burkina Faso (West Africa), when Oxfam assisted local communities in expanding their use of stone lines, crop yields increased by over 50 percent in some instances. Such systems also trap soil, helping reduce erosion, especially when they are used on sloping land or in areas where soil is especially vulnerable to erosion.

Maintaining or extending forest cover is another way of harvesting water, since the forests store rainwater and then release it gradually into the water system. Where forest cover has been removed (deforestation), downstream rivers have suffered regular shortages of water. In Kenya, for example, deforestation is blamed for rivers and fields drying up

Simple stone lines, shown here in Burkina Faso, demonstrate the technique of water harvesting.

A concrete surface traps and stores rainwater in Lanzarote, in the Canary Islands.

FACT

Rainwater from the roof of the Millennium Dome in London was collected and used to flush the toilets around the exhibition site.

around the town of Nakuru. Many are now campaigning against further loss of trees, as forested land provides around 90 percent of Kenya's domestic water and much of its irrigation capacity.

Meanwhile, in South Africa, the government is actively encouraging the removal of trees and bushes close to streams and rivers. This is because it wants to increase the amount of water flowing downstream for human consumption, and prevent its being absorbed by trees and other vegetation.

A Conservation Ethic

As water resources become scarcer, we will all have to look at ways of conserving existing supplies. Everyone can do his or her part—by using less water, improving water efficiency, and making the most of what is naturally available. We can even harvest water around our own homes, using a rain barrel placed under a downspout, to collect rainwater that falls on our roofs and would normally be wasted. This water is perfectly good for uses such as watering plants or lawns. In general, people need to start thinking twice before they turn on the faucet.

VIEWPOINT

"It's a suicidal mission, to interfere with them [forests] is to interfere with the rain system, the water system, and therefore agriculture, not to mention the other industries that are dependent on hydroelectricity."
Wangari Maathai, head of the Green Belt Movement advocacy group, Kenya

DEBATE

What methods could you use to conserve water in and around your own home or school? How might you encourage others to use similar methods?

WATER CONFLICTS

The Water Boils Over!

As water grows scarce, it is increasingly becoming the subject of conflict. Such conflicts have already occurred at international, national, and local levels, and some experts have suggested that water disputes could even lead to war in parts of the world. Others believe that talk of war is exaggerated, but most agree that conflicts over water are likely to become more common and should be taken seriously. Water issues in several locations have already boiled over into conflict.

Local disputes

Much water conflict tends to be limited to local or regional disputes. In California, for example, armed guards were sent to protect water head-gates after farmers, angry at reductions in their irrigation allowance, succeeded in breaking them down during the summer of 2001. In Kenya, meanwhile, a dispute between herders and farmers over access to a water point on the Tana River turned violent in early 2001, resulting in the death of 15 people. Similar conflicts between herders and farmers have been reported throughout the world, as traditional watering holes used by herders (sometimes for hundreds of years) are exploited by farmers for irrigation to meet the increased demand for food.

Refugees in Bangladesh patiently wait in line for water. Tensions can mount if supplies run short.

The Narmada Dam, India—a cause of great conflict over water resources between the government and local communities.

Perhaps some of the most serious local disputes involve the construction of dams. Dams are normally built for flood protection, water storage, irrigation, or generating hydroelectric power (HEP), and sometimes for a combination of reasons. Small dams have a fairly insignificant effect on people and the environment, but large dams have led to the loss of land, the flooding of communities, and the destruction of livelihoods that may have existed for thousands of years.

Current controversial projects include the Three Gorges Dam on the Yangtze river in China and the Narmada project in India. These projects will result in millions of people losing their land, and they have led to protests by local villagers and community groups. With the benefit of modern communications, these local disputes have become global debates and caused governments and international financial organizations to consider withdrawing funding for such projects. In 1997, people affected by dam projects from throughout the world met in Curitiba, Brazil, and agreed on a declaration against such projects.

VIEWPOINT

"It is both necessary and possible to bring an end to the era of destructive dams. It is also both necessary and possible to implement alternative ways of providing energy and managing our freshwaters which are equitable, sustainable, and effective."
Dam-affected signatories of the Curitiba Declaration, 1997

National Disputes

At a national level, dams have also caused disputes between different users of water. Because dams change the natural flow of rivers, they disrupt the movement of nutrients and fish. In Egypt, for example, the Aswan Dam now blocks the once annual flood of nutrient-rich sediment that used to provide farmers in the Nile valley and the delta with some of the most fertile farmland in the world. As a result, farmers have been forced to use chemical fertilizers, which in turn have led to higher levels of water pollution in downstream areas.

Fisheries have been affected in many countries. In France two dams across the Loire river were demolished in 1998–1999, to help restore the damaged fishing industry. Meanwhile, the United States, which has over 70,000 dams, has also begun removing dams that disrupt fisheries or cause other environmental problems.

International Disputes

Almost half the world's population relies on water from rivers that cross international boundaries. The countries involved have to reach agreements over their entitlement to water supplies, and such situations can lead to great tension. This pressure is felt especially in the Middle East, which is one of the driest regions on Earth. The mouth of the Nile is in the Middle Eastern country of Egypt (itself often referred to as "the gift of the Nile" because of its dependence on the river for its water needs). But the river flows through nine other countries besides Egypt, and tensions over their varied water demands have been growing for many years.

In 1979, for example, Egypt threatened to attack Ethiopia if it proceeded with plans to withdraw water from the Blue Nile by building new dams. The Blue Nile supplies around 70 percent of the water flowing into the Nile in Egypt, and any reduction in this amount would be disastrous for the Egyptians and their economy. Ethiopia, however, only uses around 3 percent of the water flowing into the Nile. With population growth among the highest in the world, Ethiopia considers greater access to Nile water essential for its development.

Egypt's dependence on the shared waters of the Nile has led it to the brink of war with neighboring countries.

This desalination plant in Iraq was destroyed by the U.N., to pressure the government into accepting international agreements.

Overcoming Conflict

Because water is such an essential resource, it is important that conflicts over its use be resolved. However, it is precisely because water is so important that such agreements can be difficult to reach, as each user often believes it has a right to the disputed water.

One way to overcome water conflicts is to increase the supply of water by using new sources (such as untapped aquifers) or constructing desalination plants. As we have seen, however, groundwater extraction is often unsustainable and desalination is currently very expensive. Improved water conservation techniques can also reduce the pressure of conflicts by using water more efficiently and therefore making more available for competing users. The problem is that many of the areas where conflict over water is most likely, such as the Middle East, already use water more efficiently than regions where it is plentiful, and so there is often little room for further improvement.

Water Agreements

Where conflict cannot be resolved by finding more water or using less, the only solution is for the various users to come to an agreement about how much each of them uses. Many such agreements exist all over the world. For example, many irrigation projects only allow farmers to extract an agreed amount of water, and they have to extract it on specific days. If farmers take more than their fair

VIEWPOINTS

"Egypt will never tolerate or accept the construction of any projects that affect the flow of the Nile or the amount of water reaching the Egyptian part of the Nile."
Dr. Awad el Moor, Egyptian Supreme Court judge

"This watershed agreement reflects the new spirit of cooperation between the countries of the Nile."
Mr. Shiferaw Jarso, minister of water resources, Ethiopia, 2001

share, they can be punished. But it is difficult to monitor such agreements, and farmers at the end of irrigation networks ("tail-enders") frequently suffer from water shortages because of overextraction by those farther up.

Agreements over water taken from rivers are even harder to enforce. Nevertheless, one successful agreement has been that between Egypt and Sudan, signed in 1959, to say how much water each would extract from the Nile. However, as other Nile countries increased their demands, the water levels in the river came under threat. New agreements between all the nations sharing the Nile basin (the river and its drainage area) have been signed in recent years, and it is hoped that these will help resolve future water conflicts in the region. Other countries are watching carefully to see how well it will work.

DEBATE

Thinking about the water supply in your local area, what sort of issues do you think could lead to conflict? How might such conflicts be resolved? Whose opinions should be considered?

The ancient temple of Abu Simbel in southern Egypt was relocated to save it from the rising waters of Lake Nasser behind the Aswan Dam. The dam assures Egypt's water supplies.

A NEW WATER ECONOMY

Paying for Water

Central to any debate about the future of water supplies is the amount people pay for water. Everyone pays for water in some way. Most people living in more developed countries pay a service provider, such as a water company or the government. The system is often similar in the towns and cities of less developed countries, but in the rural areas many people collect free water from local sources like streams. However, they still pay for their water—with time rather than money. Collecting enough water for the household can take several hours, and this prevents them from carrying out other tasks that could be generating income. Women and children are particularly affected, and may have to walk many miles each day to collect water.

For these communities, having a source of water closer to the home would not only help improve people's health. It would also give them more time, which would enable them to earn more money and improve their standard of living. But who will pay to bring water to such communities? Water companies will only invest in such systems if they can make money, but poorer communities may not be able to afford to pay for water.

Willing to Pay

In fact, there is evidence to suggest that even the poorest communities are willing to pay for improvements in water supply and quality, especially if water-related diseases cause them to spend time away from work or their education due to sickness.

Many also recognize that the time they spend collecting or treating water is very costly. In Dehradun city, in the Uttar Pradesh region of India, a 1996 study showed that people were willing to pay more than twice what they then paid for water supplies. Likewise, in rural Kerala state, people were willing to pay up to five times as much to see improved supplies and water quality. These Indian examples suggest that companies or governments could invest in improving water systems, knowing that people were willing to pay for the improvements. In reality, however, it is not so simple.

FACT

Friends of the Earth believes water companies should pay ten times the current rate for water extractions in order to promote greater efficiency.

Many people in developing countries may spend several hours each day collecting water.

FACT

In the United States, in 1997, a 10 percent increase in the price of water was found to reduce agricultural demand by 4–7 percent and urban residential demand by 3–12 percent.

VIEWPOINT

"...increased developing world indebtedness has meant there are limited amounts of finance available to governments to improve water supplies and sanitation...."
WaterAid

Subsidized Water

In many countries, the price consumers pay for government-provided water and sanitation is actually lower than the cost of providing those services. This is because governments see water and sanitation as a basic right and they therefore help to fund water and sanitation facilities in their country. Such payments are known as subsidies.

However, if the government is using its funds to subsidize existing services, there is normally little (if any) money left for expansion, improvement, or maintenance. Customers also get used to paying low prices for water and this can encourage inefficiency and wastefulness. The wealthy (who can most easily afford to pay the real price for water) tend to benefit most from subsidies because they are connected to the subsidized systems. Poorer individuals and communities who are not connected have to buy water from private sources

German experts provide a safe water supply during floods in Dhaka, Bangladesh. Such emergency supplies are invaluable.

or small-scale vendors and often pay many times more for it. In Istanbul, Turkey, for example, the poor pay ten times more for their water than those connected to the main city service and in Jakarta, capital of Indonesia, and Karachi, Pakistan, the difference in cost is up to sixty times!

Water Privatization

Many governments and organizations now recognize that subsidizing water is rarely effective and that private water companies can play an increasingly important role. Others are concerned, however, that these companies will run water services for profit and that poor people may not be able to afford sufficient water to meet their needs.

In Bolivia, the privatization of the water system in the city of Cochabamba led to riots after the new company raised water prices by 35 percent without showing any improvement in services. Water bills were equal to a third of people's average income and, because water in the city was now privately owned, it was even necessary to apply for a permit to collect rainwater from your own roof. Eventually, the Bolivian government was forced to end its contract with the water company; but in the capital, La Paz, a French water company has been more successful. They agreed to connect every house in the city to the water system by 2002, allowing poorer people to pay for the initial connection by helping with the construction of the project rather than with money. The project in La Paz may prove to be a success, but there are many places where privatization is raising the cost of water. This means that the poorest members of society can no longer afford the water they need. For example, plans to privatize water in Ghana, Africa, are being opposed by local communities. In Accra, the capital, activists say that ten buckets of water could cost almost half the daily minimum wage if privatization goes ahead.

FACT

In less developed nations, 25 percent of people living in cities pay 10–20 percent of their income for water from private vendors.

VIEWPOINT

"Public water and sanitation services are often plagued by inefficiency, which drives up service costs, restricts coverage, and leads either to needlessly high tariffs or equally needless subsidies."
World Bank, Water Sanitation and Poverty, 2001

Sustainable Pricing

In some parts of the world, wealthy people currently pay less per unit for the water to fill their luxury swimming pools than others living nearby who buy drinking water from private vendors. One possible way of resolving such inequalities would be to introduce what the Great Britain's Department For International Development (DFID) has called a "lifeline tariff." This would set a low charge for water needed to meet basic needs and a higher rate for all water used beyond that basic requirement. Those who chose to have swimming pools or to water their gardens with wasteful sprinklers would be forced to pay for such luxuries. The higher-rate tax would also encourage people not to waste water, and help build a more sustainable water economy.

Many poor communities pay more for bottled water than the rich do for piped water. These vendors are in Darjeeling, India.

Hydrogen Boost

The hydrogen fuel cell could be a major factor in developing the new water economy. This technological breakthrough uses hydrogen in powerful fuel cells that could soon be powering vehicles—in place of gasoline or diesel engines. The cells are already in use in some buses in Canada where they were first developed, and several major car manufacturers, such as Ford, Honda, and Mercedes Benz, hope to start using them in cars before 2010.

There is excitement about the potential of hydrogen fuel cells, particularly as the hydrogen needed could be extracted from water (made up of hydrogen and oxygen), using a process called electrolysis.

Electrolysis separates hydrogen from water and releases pollution-free oxygen as a waste product. In the fuel cells, the hydrogen is recombined with oxygen (from the air) and generates electricity for powering the vehicle, with water vapor as the only emission. The problem is that electrolysis requires a lot of energy, but if renewable energy sources were used—such as the solar power being used at an experimental plant in Barcelona—then it would be possible to have near pollution-free cars.
Using water as a fuel would admittedly increase

VIEWPOINTS

"The key to raising water productivity is pricing water at its market value."
Lester Brown, Worldwatch Institute

"Water is not a [tradable] good, it is a resource that needs to be managed."
Pierre Pettigrew, Canadian trade minister

Traders concerned about the price of oil. Such concern is rarely shown for water, but perhaps it should be!

demand on water supplies. However, water might then become "the new oil," in what some are already calling a "sustainable hydrogen economy." This could lead to water being recognized as a more valuable resource, and therefore greater efforts might be made to conserve it.

DEBATE

Why is water often priced lower than its real value? If you had to increase the price to cover the real cost of treating and supplying water to people's homes, how would you explain the increase to them?

WATER FOR TOMORROW

Urgent Action

The fact that water is increasingly a focus of attention for international organizations and national governments is welcomed by those

Harvesting mist in Chile is an innovative way of improving water supplies.

concerned with water supply and sanitation issues. But while they discuss the best way to manage, conserve, and protect water, the number of people living without access to even the most basic water supplies continues to rise. If present trends continue, two-thirds of the world's population will live in countries suffering from water stress by the year 2025. These startling statistics are making some world leaders call for urgent action today. They tell us there is no time to wait for technological solutions, such as improved irrigation, or for governments and private companies to invest in new systems. The time for action is now, but what type of action?

A Water Package
In reality, there is no single action that can quickly resolve water supply problems, but a combination of different measures could have rapid and far-reaching effects.
- Simple educational messages, such as teaching people to wash their hands and to boil water before drinking it, have been proven to have an immediate effect on the number of people suffering from water-related disease.
- Repairing pipes could immediately reduce the 30 percent of water leaking from many networks.

FACT

Since 1980, more than 2.4 billion people have gained access to a water supply and 600 million to sanitation.

- Creating and, more importantly, enforcing laws against pollution could make existing water supplies safer for human consumption.
- Simple conservation measures, such as replacing old toilets with new low-flow toilets, have proven very effective in improving water supplies.

These are just some of the actions that could be taken relatively quickly, but perhaps the most effective strategy would be to change people's long-term attitude to water.

Personal Behavior and Attitudes

For the millions who rise with the sun to collect enough water to see them through the day, the value of water is clear. For millions of others (probably including yourself), the fact that they must simply turn the faucet on in their homes to obtain seemingly endless supplies of water leads them to take water for granted. Politicians, business leaders, and decision-makers are often included in this latter group, and so they, too, may not give water the priority it deserves.

VIEWPOINTS

"Two decades ago less than half the people of the developing world had access to safe, clean water. Now more than two-thirds have this most fundamental resource."
A to Z of World Development, published by New Internationalist magazine, 1998

"Despite our progress, half of the world's population still suffers with water services inferior to those available to the ancient Greeks and Romans."
Peter Gleick, director, Pacific Institute for Studies in Development, Environment, and Security, 2001

Protecting forests also helps to protect water supplies.

VIEWPOINTS

"We cannot stand idly back when we know that 1.2 billion people throughout the planet's developing countries still enjoy no adequate access to safe sources of freshwater. Twice as many are yet denied access to proper sanitation services."
Koïchiro Matsuura, director-general, United Nations Educational, Scientific, and Cultural Organization (UNESCO)

"Clearly, a problem of this magnitude cannot be solved overnight, but simple, inexpensive measures, both individual and collective, are available that will provide clean water for millions and millions of people in developing countries—now, not in 10 or 20 years."
Gro Harlem Brundtland, director-general, World Health Organization

It is vital for the long-term future of water supplies that all people realize the value of this most basic resource and change their behavior accordingly. We have discussed the simple changes that most of us can make in and around our homes, but it is important that schools, businesses, and industries also take such measures. Furthermore, those in positions of authority should re-examine their practices to look for ways of improving water efficiency, reducing waste, and avoiding pollution. Governments should consider financial incentives, such as the introduction of water meters, higher water charges, pollution taxes, or subsidies on water-saving technology. Such changes might be unpopular because many see water as a basic right and for many years have paid an artificially low price for the water they use. However, if the targets of universal clean water, safe sanitation, and environmental protection are to be met over the coming decades, there may be no choice but to take such measures.

A Sustainable Future?

At the start of this book, we saw how little of the water covering our planet is actually available for human use. Human pressure is reducing this amount every day—threatening the survival not only of

In 2000, Lake Rajsamand in India dried up for the first time in living history: a stark warning of a water-scarce future.

future generations of humans, but also of precious aquatic environments. To create a sustainable future, we need to reverse these patterns, seeking to provide sufficient water for all people while protecting supplies and the environment for future generations. Such a challenge is not simple, but processes such as global climate change (which is itself affecting the amount of water available in some places) sound a warning to those who choose to ignore the issues and continue with "business as usual."

Whether or not the human race rises to the challenge depends on the individuals, including you and me, who benefit from the wealth of the world's resources. Showing that we are aware of water supply issues and willing to take action to resolve them sends positive signals to our families, friends, and governments alike. Water, along with the air we breathe, is a basic requirement for our survival. So it is certainly our shared responsibility to make sure that the right to clean water and safe sanitation becomes a reality for the people of the world—now and in the future.

Many still use water as though it is free and plentiful; such attitudes have to change.

FACT

March 22 is designated as "World Water Day"— an annual day to raise awareness of water-supply issues around the globe.

DEBATE

Having learned more about water supply in the early 21st century, what do you believe should be the priorities for those in charge of managing future water supplies?

GLOSSARY

aquatic living, growing, or taking place in/on water.

aquifer a store of water contained within rock formations, often sandstone or limestone. Much of the world's population relies on aquifers for their water supply. They dig wells to reach the stored water.

bunds small ridges created to help conserve water and/or prevent soil erosion. They are often used across sloping land where erosion and run-off are greatest.

condensation process whereby a substance turns from a gas to a liquid. For example, water vapor condenses within clouds to form precipitation.

Curitiba Declaration a statement of people affected by dam projects, signed in Curitiba, Brazil, in 1997.

DDT the abbreviation for Dichloro-Diphenyl-Trichloroethane, an insecticide used to kill mosquitoes. It has harmful side effects in people, animals, and fish. It is now banned in many countries but is still used in some developing countries.

deforestation the removal of trees, shrubs, and forest vegetation. This can be natural (due to forest fires, typhoons, etc.) or a result of human action (logging, ranching, construction, land clearance, etc.).

desalination the removal of salt from water (usually seawater) to make it into fresh-water for drinking or other uses.

developed countries the wealthier countries of the world, including Europe, North America, Japan, Australia, and New Zealand. People living there are normally healthy, well-educated, and work in a wide variety of high-technology industries.

developing countries the poorer countries of the world, sometimes called the Third World and including most of Africa, Asia, Latin America, and Oceania. People living there are often unhealthy, poorly educated, and work in agriculture and low-technology industries.

ecosystem the contents of an environment, including all the plants and animals that live there. This could be a garden pond, a forest, or all of planet Earth.

eutrophication a process whereby water becomes enriched with nutrients that encourage rapid algae and plant growth. It can result in mats of plants that block out the sunlight and starve the water of oxygen, leading to the death of aquatic animals.

evaporation the process whereby water is converted to a gas or vapor.

freshwater water that contains less than 0.2 percent salt.

glacier a mass of ice and snow normally found in mountainous or polar regions. As glaciers move and break up, they melt and flow into streams, rivers, or groundwater.

groundwater water that lies beneath the ground, but above an impermeable (water cannot pass through it) layer of rock. Groundwater comes mainly from rain that percolates through the soil and permeable rocks.

habitat the place in which an animal or plant lives. For example, a squirrel lives in a woodland habitat.

hydrosphere all the water found on Earth's surface, including water in the soil, groundwater, ice, and snow.

interdependent two or more factors that depend on one another.

irrigation the artificial application of water to crops to compensate for low or unpredictable rainfall.

leachate a solution or product obtained by removing harmful elements from the soil.

nitrates salts of nitric acid used in agricultural fertilizers, food preservatives, and explosives. Nitrates can contribute to eutrophication if they enter the water system.

Oceania the lands of the central and South Pacific, including Micronesia, Melanesia, Polynesia (New Zealand), often Australia, and sometimes the Malay Archipelago.

percolation the downward seepage of water through pores and joints in the soil and rock.

phosphates salts of phosphoric acid used in some agricultural fertilizers and household cleaning products, such as laundry soaps.

pit latrine basic toilet above a deep hole or "pit" in the ground, rather than one that is connected to a sewage system.

precipitation water from the atmosphere that is deposited as rain, snow, dew, hail, or sleet on Earth's surface.

privatized when a national property is sold to a company or individuals to be privately owned and managed.

rain barrel a barrel used for collecting rainwater as it flows from a roof and is diverted from the rainspout.

river basin the total area of land drained by a river and its tributaries.

saltwater intrusion the contamination of freshwater supplies by saltwater. Normally caused by overextraction of aquifers in coastal regions.

sanitation hygienic toilets and washing facilities to prevent the spread of diseases associated with human waste.

sewage waste carried by sewers for treatment or disposal. Sewage includes human waste and waste water, as well as chemicals from homes, offices, and factories.

snowfield an area of permanent snow with a level and fairly smooth surface, like a field.

surface run-off the movement of water down a slope after heavy precipitation.

tail-enders farmers with land located toward the end of an irrigation system who are likely to suffer water shortages due to extraction further up.

transpiration the loss of water vapor through a plant's pores into the atmosphere, which contributes to the formation of clouds.

tubewell a well dug or drilled to reach deep water resources and then lined with a pipe or tube.

waste water water that has been previously used for domestic, industrial, or agricultural purposes and is returned into the water system.

water cycle the continuous circulation of water between hydrosphere and atmosphere.

water harvesting collecting water for human use. This normally involves using a storage method (e.g., a rain barrel) or a barrier (e.g., bunds) to capture rainfall.

watershed a line of high ground separating two river basins (the total area of land drained by a river).

water table a level in the ground below which water is found. It can move up or down depending on how much rain has fallen and the rate of water extraction.

yield the total amount of crops grown in a measured area (normally an acre) per year.

BOOKS TO READ

McLeish, Ewan. *Protecting Our Planet: Keeping Water Clean*. New York: Raintree Steck-Vaughn Publishers, 1998.

Morgan, Sally. *Earth Watch: Water for All*. Franklin Watts Inc., 2000.

Ocko, Stephanie. *Water: Almost Enough for Everyone*. Atheneum, 1995.

Tesar, Jenny. *Food and Water: Threats, Shortages, and Solutions (Our Fragile Planets)*. Facts on File Inc., 1992.

USEFUL ADDRESSES

Friends of the Earth
1025 Vermont Avenue, N.W.
Washington, DC 20005
Tel: (877) 843-8687

The National Water and Climate Center
101 S.W. Main Street, Suite 1600
Portland, OR 97204
Tel: (503) 414-3107

U.S. Environmental Protection Agency
Office of Water (4101M)
1200 Pennsylvania Avenue, N.W.
Washington, DC 20460

The National Water and Climate Center
www.wcc.nrcs.usda.gov/wcc.html
This division of the National Resources Conservation Service, which is an agency of the United States Department of Agriculture, provides water supply forecasts as well as information on water quality and quantity.

Water Supply and Sanitation Collaborative Council
www.wsscc.org
Dedicated to ensuring water, sanitation, and hygiene for all, this organization aims to improve water sanitation and management services to the world's poor.

Water Conservation and Efficiency
www.mwra.state.ma.us/water/html/cons.htm

INDEX

Numbers in **bold** refer to illustrations.